Poison Cream

Volume 1

Collection of Poems

Laura Strangers

Title: Poison Cream Volume 1

Author: Laura Strangers

First edition: October 2023

Turn Turn

In a golden field under the summer sky,

A sunflower rises, blazing and alive.

With his yellow face, he smiles in the sun,

An ancient bond, a love without words.

Elegant and proud, in the wind it bends,

But it never breaks, its strength does not deny.

Round and round, it follows the divine light,

An eternal dance, a morning dance.

Its green leaves, like outstretched hands,

They welcome the warmth, in a hanging embrace.

And in the brown heart, a life hides,

Seeds of hope, in a deep circle.

Symbol of fidelity, of constant love,

The sunflower teaches with a radiant gaze:

To look for light, even on dark days,

To tend to the sun when life runs away.

And when the sunset paints the sky orange,

The sunflower bows, in a sincere greeting.

He waits for the dawn, with endless hope,

A new day, a new life.

So in the sunflower, in that burning corolla,

It hides a message, simple and powerful:

Be constant in your love, be faithful to your sun,

And life will surprise you, with a wonderful dance.

Zumo

Another day

in the trenches

Randomly thrown rhymes

To narrate

this epic.

It is cold

I turn on

The heating

I look at the pc

Yet another customer

wants reimbursement:

No comment.

Another day

in the trenches

Randomly thrown rhymes

To narrate

this epic.

Like the Titanic

We are going downhill

Pausing the fork

In the paste I shove.

Sparrow

In the green garden, in the gentle morning,

A small sparrow perched on the path.

The glittering feathers, the shining eyes,

A light song, a vibrant flight.

Under the blue sky, among the flowering branches,

He danced in the wind, without endless thoughts.

In its fragile wings, freedom found,

In nature he was lost, with joy he sang.

In a world of birch trees and quiet valleys,

The sparrow taught, without saying words, his dances.

A call to life, a sigh of love,

A silent message from his heart.

Man, observer, rapt and enchanted,

By that creature he felt called.

In its light flight, a profound lesson,

A subtle teaching about respecting the world.

Thus in the song of the sparrow, simple and pure,

It hides wisdom, the love of the future.

Look at the little bird, let it guide you,

In nature you will find peace, love, a new look to admire.

Moth and hare

In the ancient forest, in a distant time,
A vain hare, a bold and insane step,
He challenged in competition, with laughter and mockery,
A wise tortoise, steady-footed and tern.

"You slow and clumsy, me quick and slender,
How can you hope to win, O little maiden?"
Said the hare, jumping high and carefree,
The turtle looked at her, serene and focused.

"I accept the challenge," he replied calmly,
"My pace is slow, but constant is the soul,
It is not speed that determines victory,
But constancy, patience, and ardent glory."

Thus began the race, under the eye of the sun,
The hare sprinted, the tortoise without a flight,
Step by step, without hurry or fatigue,
The turtle advanced with firm certainty.

The hare, confident, stopped to rest,

"This race is mine," he thought, without wading,

But as he slept, in the golden dream,

The turtle advanced, the finish line approached.

At the end of the day, when the shadow grows larger,

The hare woke up, feeling a fierce loss,

He ran, he jumped, but it was too late,

The turtle had won, with its firm, late pace.

In the simple story of hare and tortoise,

A truth is concealed, a sharp lesson:

It is not speed or arrogance that pays,

But perseverance, patience, and a wise mind.

Memories

In the silent rooms of the soul,

Memories reside, endless shadows,

Echoes of moments, footprints on the path,

Whispers of yesterday in a sincere heart.

Some are lights, stars in the night,

They guide and comfort when the road becomes broken,

Memories of love, friends and joy,

Sparks of a time, which never bores.

Others are shadows, melancholy mists,

Regrets and longings, ironic memories,

They leave a taste, sometimes bitter,

But they also teach on this bizarre journey.

Between the yellowed pages, in an old album,

Faces are concealed, of a time never tamed,

Smiles and tears, in a faded photo,

A past world, an endless life.

Each memory is a bridge, a deep connection,

With what we were, in a distant second,

An invitation to look, with wise and serene eyes,

The plot woven, by our fates.

In the dance of memories, in the light melody,

We find ourselves again, in an embrace that does not encumber,

An invitation to remember, with love and care,

Every step lived, in this adventure.

Thus, when the evening comes, the mind becomes quiet,

And memories return, like secret breezes,

Welcome them warmly, in a sincere smile,

I am an echo of you, your true past.

Wet and dry

On the golden shoreline, where the sea kisses the land,

Summer flares up, in a sincere dance,

Waves whisper promise, on the light wind,

Sun caresses the skin, in an embrace of pleasure.

Children laugh and play, sand castles erect,

Innocence and magic, in their world are lost,

Surfers ride the waves, sailors brave the wind,

Summer by the sea, an eternal moment.

The eyes are lost, in the infinite horizon,

Where the sky kisses the water, in a deep connection,

Dreams and hopes, floating in the salty air,

Time suspended, memory that never recedes.

Summer loves are born, under shining stars,

Stolen kisses, burning promises,

Fires on the beach, guitars playing,

Stories and songs, which the heart tunes.

Seagulls glide, in the clear blue sky,

Freedom in flight, a rare song,

Shells whisper secrets, in the palm of your hand,

Mysteries of the sea, in a distant embrace.

Summer by the sea, an ancient and true ritual,

Return to the essence, a sincere breath,

In the saltiness and heat, in the rustle of the wave,

One finds life again, a deep connection.

Thus, when winter advances, cold and severe,

It calls to the heart, that sincere sea,

The summer lived, the sun, the froth,

A golden memory, a melody that smells.

Soprano

Around the big table, in a cozy room,

The family gathers, in a sweet and smiling moment,

Father, mother, children, grandparents, in a circle of love,

Food, laughter, and warmth are shared.

Hands prepare, in the laborious kitchen,

Fragrant dishes, tasty recipes,

Each dish is a language, a sincere message,

A bond, a history, a true affection.

They sit and look at each other, eyes bright and content,

Thanks is given for the food, for the love present,

Cutlery dances, glasses toast,

Hearts open, souls embrace.

Stories intertwine, between bites and smiles,

Memories go back up, in purposeful dialogue,

Generations come together, in that ancient ritual,

The family meal, a unique and friendly time.

Children laugh, adults tell stories,

Grandparents whisper wisdoms, eyes meet,

In that simple act, of eating together,

It hides the universe, a redeeming love.

And when the meal ends, and the dishes gather,

There remains a warmth, a joy that does not escape,

Because shared food, in a united family,

It is more than nourishment; it is the essence of life.

So, if you look closely, in that common scene,

You will find a treasure, an opportune melody,

The family at the table in a serene embrace,

It is a picture of love, an eternal portrait.

Don't stop believing

On the cold sidewalk, under an unlit streetlight,

A girl waits, her face serious and intent,

Evening advances, with its long shadows,

The train approaches, a fate that eludes.

The suitcase at his side, heavy with dreams and hopes,

His eyes fixed on the tracks in a dance of circumstance,

Where is he going? Who is he? What is he looking for in that race?

Every journey is a mystery, a hidden promise.

The train whistles, stops with a sigh,

Doors open, a future still unknown,

The girl goes up, with a firm step,

In that silent carriage, an imprecise world.

The windows show fast-fading landscapes,

Cities and fields, light and shadow, in imaginative play,

The girl looks outside, her heart in turmoil,

A farewell, a beginning, a path never traveled.

Who awaits her at the other end? What adventure awaits her?

In that night race, every soul is secret,

The girl in the train, an enigmatic figure,

An unwritten story, a harmonic melody.

And when the train disappears into the deep night,

There remains an echo, a memory, a deep question,

Every journey is a poem, every farewell a song,

Every fate a mystery, every heart an enchantment.

Thus, in the girl who takes the train in the evening,

It hides humanity, a sincere beauty,

A passage, a transition, a courageous flight,

A love of life, a silent dream.

Bananas

In a tropical orchard, under a blazing sun,

It grows a banana, yellow and smiling,

Curved and shimmering, in a brilliant dress,

An exotic fruit, an inviting flavor.

It is born green, shy, in a leafy embrace,

It slowly matures into a sunny kiss,

It turns yellow and sweet, ready to be picked,

A natural delight, a blazing wonder.

Open its peel, with a sincere gesture,

It reveals its essence, in a light smile,

Tender and juicy, a taste that dances,

A banana is a treat, a sweet hope.

On the breakfast plate, or in a quick snack,

She is a faithful friend, a suave and flourishing companion,

In a cake, in a smoothie, or just alone,

A banana is a joy, a melody that flies.

It is not only a fruit, but a curious symbol,

Of exoticism and travel, of a mysterious world,

A connection with the earth, with nature that creates,

A banana is an art, a sculpture that cheers.

So the next time you take a banana,

Look at it with new eyes, with an arcane vision,

In that yellow curve, in that suave flavor,

You'll find a poem, a love that won't go away.

Sunset

On the edge of the day, where the sun declines,

One paints the sunset, in a divine work,

A harmony of colors, a heavenly ballet,

A sweet and calm farewell, a masterful moment.

Red and gold merge, in a fiery embrace,

Purple and pink whisper, in a vibrant kiss,

The sky ignites, in a song of love,

Sunset is an art, a color and a smell.

The sun goes down, with a regal gesture,

It disappears over the horizon in a final salute,

It leaves behind, a brilliant trace,

A memory, a wish, an elegant sigh.

The trees stand out, in a dark profile,

They watch the sunset in pure silence,

The sea reflects colors, in an eternal mirror,

A play of light, a sincere embrace.

Birds fly home in a light dance,

The world prepares, for the night that weaves,

Sunset is a bridge, between day and evening,

A moment of peace, a sincere beauty.

Look at that sunset, with the eyes of the soul,

You will find a poem, a calm melody,

An invitation to reflect, to give thanks, to dream,

An eternal image that never ceases to enchant.

Each sunset is unique, a gift, a gift,

A sign of nature, a love that is never dull,

Thus, when the sun goes down, and the day closes,

Remember that there is beauty in those nuances.

Sisters

Your sisters

They are not capable

Of sewing

And I can't help you

If you stay behind

With work.

Don't hang around

If you deliver

Late

Then the clerk

About the store

He scolds you

And you make a fool of yourself

In front of customers.

Moreover,

Your boss

He doesn't pay you.

Your sisters

They are not capable

Of sewing

And I can't help you

If you stay behind

With work.

Don't hang around

If you deliver

Late

Then the clerk

About the store

He scolds you

And you make a fool of yourself

In front of customers.

Moreover,

Your boss

He doesn't pay you.

Geese

For two geese

they walked

Their webbed paws

They were tired

Then.

They stopped at the river

And they take advantage of it

To water

Without ceasing

Of gossipping.

Gina recounted

That that bitch

About his colleague

She had made herself

impregnate

Of the first moron

On Duty

And Ornella,

Beak wide open

And wide eyes,

He didn't miss a word.

For two geese

they walked

Their webbed paws

They were tired

Then.

They stopped at the river

And they take advantage of it

To water

Without ceasing

Of gossipping.

Gina recounted

That that bitch

About his colleague

She had made herself

impregnate

Of the first moron

On Duty

And Ornella,

Beak wide open

And wide eyes,

He didn't miss a word.

Among the waves

In a wave embrace, under an endless sky,

A glass bottle, travels in the thin sea,

Snake in the waves, dancing with the current,

A closed message, a pending fate.

Who launched it? What secret does it hold?

A lost love, a sincere hope?

In that shiny glass, in that tight cap,

An enigma is hidden, a perfect love.

The stars look at her, the sun kisses her,

The wind propels it, on a daring adventure,

It goes from island to island, from beach to reef,

A wandering bottle, a sincere siren.

Perhaps there is a letter inside, with handwritten words,

Perhaps a drawing, a distant dream,

Maybe just a memory, a scent, a trace,

Of those who entrusted her, to that daring dance.

Someday, perhaps, on the shore it will rest,

A passerby will find it, the cap will open,

He will read that message, hear that voice,

Of a distant stranger, of a grazing heart.

Or perhaps it will continue, on its endless journey,

A bottle in the sea, a love that never ended,

A symbol of hope, courage and faith,

A connection to the human, a melody that asks.

Thus, if you look at the sea, with curious eyes,

He thinks about that bottle, his precious dreams,

Each wave could carry, a message, a sign,

Everlasting love, serene embrace.

The bottle in the sea, a poetic image,

A call to adventure, to a world without rhetoric,

A bridge between strangers, a thin thread,

A story never told, a fragile song.

Karma

In an intricate fabric of choices and destinies,
It unwinds karma, in divine paths,
Every action, an echo, every thought, a seed,
A silent law, a pressing order.

He does not judge, punish, smile or cry,
Karma moves, without a face, without a strange label,
It is a flow, a rhythm, a cosmic dance,
A connection between the whole, a harmonic truth.

Plant love, and love will flourish,
Sow hatred, and hatred will grow,
Every gesture is reflected, in a mirror universe,
A returning wave, a vibrant energy.

It is not revenge, it is not prize, it is just balance,
A balance of forces, a subtle and serious dialogue,
Each heart is a node, in a timeless network,
Each life is a chapter, in a windless book.

Seek goodness, live wisely,

Karma will guide you, with kindness and firmness,

Be sincere, be kind, be humble and be grateful,

Your path will be clear, your destiny will be adorned.

Reflect on karma, with open eyes and a pure heart,

You will find guidance, a sure beacon,

It is life that responds, it is life that asks,

It is a universal embrace, it is a love that grants.

Karma is a poem, a song without end,

A bridge between souls, a road without lines,

Walk with awareness, listen with respect,

Karma whispers to you, your perfect destiny.

Trampled heart

In an unexpected silence, in a subtle moment,

A heart is broken, a thread is broken,

A lost love, a broken dream,

A sudden emptiness, a wheezing cry.

A broken heart, a real pain,

An open wound, a cold that knocks out,

Words are not enough, tears flow,

A farewell that burns, a memory that shakes.

Every smile is now far away, every hug is a mirage,

In the echo of that heart, a message echoes,

Of what was beautiful, of what was dear,

Now only silence remains, a bitter sweet.

In that broken heart lies a mystery,

A love that lives on, beyond sincere pain,

The cracks tell stories, of passion and faith,

Of a fire that burns, even when it is lost.

It is not the end, but a new beginning,

A broken heart is a journey, not a precipice,

There is strength in that fragility, there is beauty in that sorrow,

There is a hidden humanity, a serene truth.

Let time take in, that pain that cries out,

Let life teach, the sweet melody,

Every broken heart, is a shooting star,

A shining light, a resilient love.

So if you feel that weight, if you know that sadness,

Remember that you are whole, even in your sadness,

In every crack there is growth, in every tear there is love,

A broken heart is a poet, a dreamer.

Straight into the ravine

A dense cloud looms in the sky,
Silent and pensive, an immense enigma,
Loaded with promise, heavy with dreams,
A cloud about to rain, a dulcet melody.

A wind pushes it, cradles it, and brushes against it,
The shadows lengthen, the air becomes colored,
It is a suspended moment, a fragile moment,
A held breath, a nimble secret.

Every drop guarded, every desire hidden,
In that ready cloud, in that mysterious heart,
It is a memory of sea, it is a kiss of land,
It is an ancestral dance, it is a sincere life.

People look up, they hear that call,
That scent of rain, that distant whisper,
It is an invitation to stop, reflect and feel,
Nature speaking, life wanting to unite.

Then, in a flutter of wings, in a light rustle,

The cloud opens, in a sincere embrace,

The drops fall dancing, in an ancient ritual,

An eternal love, a melodic song.

Each drop is a caress, a touch on each leaf,

A laugh on the rooftops, a tear on the threshold,

It is life renewing, it is the earth smiling,

It is a love that welcomes, it is a poem that shines.

That raining cloud, that passing moment,

It is a profound teaching, an embracing beauty,

Every change is growth, every rain is a gift,

Each cloud is an art, a universe in a sound.

So when you see a cloud, ready to give,

Think of that miracle, that kiss that wants to come,

In every drop there is a world, in every cloud there is a heart,

Rain is a lover, a promise of love.

I wonder what you see

You turn around

With that curious little face

That you would stick everywhere

Every smell

Every flavor

A discovery that intoxicates

Your senses

Like Dali

Your mustache curls up

From trepidation.

Every now and then you stop

Enchanted

To observe a point

Of the wall,

Where I see a white wall

I wonder what you see.

You turn around

With that curious little face

That you would stick everywhere

Every smell

Every flavor

A discovery that intoxicates

Your senses

Like Dali

Your mustache curls up

From trepidation.

Every now and then you stop

Enchanted

To observe a point

About the wall,

Where I see a white wall

I wonder what you see.

Digging holes

Digging holes

Like a madman

A few days

I stumble over it

And I break a femur.

And then what do we do?

They will take me to the emergency room

Me in pain

I will swear like crazy

And with the chalk

For who knows how long

I will stay on the couch

sullen.

Digging holes

Like a madman

A few days

I stumble over it

And I break a femur.

Then what do we do?

They will take me to the emergency room

Me in pain

I will swear like crazy

And with the chalk

For who knows how long

I will stay on the couch

sullen.

Shadow

That 'vacuum cleanerIn the heart of winter, under a crystal sky,

Cold reigns, a master without mercy, without foul,

Cut the earth, embrace the bare trees,

A world in silence, a dance of fires.

Each snowflake, a perfect sculpture,

Every breath of wind, an unexpected caress,

The cold draws landscapes, with invisible hands,

Creating wonders, in impossible moments.

You walk in the cold, you feel that sincere bite,

A penetrating blade, a light kiss,

Cheeks flush, eyes light up,

In that frozen world, thoughts are purified.

The stars shine brighter on those clear nights,

The moon smiles, in that altarless cold,

Everything is naked, everything is essential,

Cold is a truth, an impartial judgment.

In homes fires are lit, hands are shaken,

Stories are told, plans are whispered,

Cold unites hearts, invites closeness,

It is a time for love; it is a time for hope.

Cold is a poet, an ageless artist,

He writes verses on the earth, sings songs on the wind,

It invites reflection, demands attention and respect,

He is a strict teacher, a discreet friend.

So when you feel the cold on a winter morning,

Greet him with a smile, with an internal embrace,

There is beauty in that frost, there is wisdom in that hand,

Cold is a gift, a human passage.

In every season there is a message, in every climate there is a
song,

Cold is a voice, a love, an enchantment,

Listen to that melody, look at that scene,

The cold is a poem, a serene magic.

Certain French expressions

Certain French expressions

I just don't understand them.

Take this one,for example:

I will translate it into Italian for you:

"I have a glass in my nose."

To say.

That I'm annoyed

for something.

That is, think if a friend

He would ask the usual question,

Thrown in there to start

Conversation,

"How are you doing?"

And you would respond:

"Mah so-so,

In this period

I have a glass in my nose!"

Think about how he would look at you.

Certain French expressions

I just don't understand them.

Take this one,for example:

I will translate it into Italian for you:

"I have a glass in my nose."

To say.

That I'm annoyed

for something.

That is, think if a friend

He would ask the usual question,

Thrown in there to start

Conversation,

"How are you doing?"

And you would respond:

"Mah so-so,

In this period

I have a glass in my nose!"

Think about how he would look at you.

The first thing

Your blond curls

They are the first thing

That I noticed about you.

Immediately after

They are

Your big eyes

Of a light green

They score

Here and there

Of yellow

Depending on the weather.

You are always sunny

Even when

Things

They look bad.

Your blond curls

They are the first thing

That I noticed about you.

Immediately after

They are

Your big eyes

Of a light green

They score

Here and there

Of yellow

Depending on the weather.

You are always sunny

Even when

Things

They look bad.

You slip into the box

You slip into the box

And you only know

How do you

To be in it all.

You

And your fluffy hair

The tail that looks like

That of a fox

Do you know what I would do with it?

A beautiful scarf

That at this rate

Given the trend

I would use as a noose.

You slip into the box

And you only know

How do you

To be in it all.

You

And your fluffy hair

The tail that looks like

That of a fox

Do you know what I would do with it?

A beautiful scarf

That at this rate

Given the trend

I would use as a noose.

Need the fan

In calloused hands, in the sweat of the forehead,
In the long hours, in the heart of a bridge,
Work is found, a fire that burns,
A struggle, a love, a melody that enchants.

He is the silent craftsman, hammer in hand,
He is the patient teacher with the book on the floor,
He is the bold farmer under the blazing sun,
He is the tireless worker in the quivering factory.

Work is a ritual, a sweet sacrifice,
A passage to the dream, a path that does not dissolve,
It is creating with the hands, it is thinking with the heart,
It is living with passion, it is seeking honor.

Each craft sings, a different song,
Each effort tells, an immersed story,
In time, in pain, in joy and in fatigue,
Work is a poem, an ancient truth.

It is not just a means, it is not just an end,

The work is a journey, an expressing love,

Who you are, what you want, where you want to go,

It is an indelible mark, a fire to embrace.

It celebrates humility, honesty and dedication,

It honors ingenuity, strength and ambition,

Work is a bond, with the land and with men,

It is a bridge between souls, a thread that illuminates.

So when you feel the burden, of a difficult day,

Remember the value, of that invisible gesture,

Every work is sacred, every craft is art,

Every effort is love, every day is a part.

Of a larger mosaic, of an endless picture,

The work is a color, in a sublime canvas,

Be proud of what you do, be grateful for every step,

The work is a gift, an embrace, an impulse.

In the hands, eyes, heart and soul,

The work lives, grows, dreams and calls,

It is an eternal song, a sincere love,

Work is life, a real journey.

Get the reindeer

Get the reindeer

And turn it

Below Above

Don't worry

If you whine a little

He certainly won't be

Just comfortable

In that position

A little forced

But quiet

That it doesn't happen to her

Nothing.

Coming up on Christmas

And together

To Santa Claus

He will bring the sled

Loaded with gifts.

Get the reindeer

And turn it

Below Above

Don't worry

If you whine a little

He certainly won't be

Just comfortable

In that position

A little forced

But quiet

That it doesn't happen to her

Nothing.

Coming up on Christmas

And together

To Santa Claus

He will bring the sled

Loaded with gifts.

Care about

In the jungle of life, in the desert of days,

Between storms and silences, beyond mountains and contours,

A rare treasure is found, an ageless diamond,

Solid friendship, a guiding light there.

It does not ask, judge, waver or break,

It is a hug that warms, a hand that caresses,

It is an attentive ear, an understanding heart,

It is a bond that grows, a love that does not end.

In shared laughter, in silent weeping,

In unspoken words, in generous gestures,

He lives solid friendship, that unparalleled bond,

A bridge between souls, a fire that burns and clear.

It does not fear time, it knows no distance,

Overcome misunderstandings, overcome all resistance,

It is an invisible force, a gentle melody,

It is an eternal dance, a crazy promise.

When the world is dark, when the way is lost,

Solid friendship is a star, a moon heard,

It is a voice that calls, it is a smile that waits,

It is a presence that remains, it is a dream that ignites.

Celebrate friendship, cherish it with care,

It is a priceless gift; it is pure beauty,

It is the answer to questions, it is the key to puzzles,

It is a comfort, a hope, an infinity of rhythms.

Be grateful for friends, for those true connections,

For those rare people, for those sincere hearts,

Solid friendship is a poem, a song without end,

It is a universal embrace, it is divine magic.

In words, in silences, in looks and in hands,

Friendship lives, talks, sings and invites tomorrow,

It is a shared joy, it is a welcomed sorrow,

Solid friendship is a love, a collected universe.

Do you want some wine?

In a bottle rests, a deep mystery,

Wine, nectar of the gods, boundless bond,

With land, with man, with weather and wave,

It is a hymn to life, a divine poem.

Color of sunset, smell of a kiss,

Taste of a memory, touch of a smile,

Wine is a journey, a suspended moment,

A hug between friends, a promised love.

In the vineyards it cradles, under the loving sun,

It grows with the rain, dances with the wind,

Each cluster tells, a story, a season,

Each glass is a world, an art, a song.

At the table brings together, families and strangers,

Toast the joys, comfort the hearts,

Wine is a language, a universal melody,

It is a shared secret, an immortal truth.

In the chalice he stirs, revealing his secrets,

Every sip is an exploration, every aroma an invitation,
To slow down, to feel, to celebrate the moment,
Wine is a master, a constant lover.

Poets and philosophers, peasants and kings,
They found in wine, a friend, a belief,
It is an ancient philosophy, an ageless beauty,
It is a living culture, a passion that goes.

So when you raise a glass, in a sincere toast,
Think about that wine, that real connection,
With life, with love, with nature and the human,
Wine is a gift, a sovereign embrace.

In color, fragrance, taste and soul,
Wine sings, speaks, dreams and calls,
It is a continuous celebration, it is a happy tear,
Wine is poetry, an art, an affecting love.

Supercar

On the asphalt ribbon, with a roar of steel,

It flows the machine, the child of ingenuity and labor,

Symbol of freedom, of power, of travel,

It is a dream on four wheels, a modern treasure.

Elegant lines draw, a moving sculpture,

Every curve is an art, every detail is precision,

The engine beats like a heart in an unstoppable dance,

The car is passion, it is speed, it is mission.

Behind the wheel one discovers, a world without boundaries,

Every road is an adventure, every journey is a discovery,

The car is a companion, in long walks,

It is a comforting embrace, an open door.

In the lights of the headlights, in the caress of the wind,

In the thrill of acceleration, in the whisper of travel,

He lives the machine, a union of technology and feeling,

An ode to innovation, a song of courage.

It is not only metal, it is not only mechanical,

The car is an expression, of wishes and dreams,

It is an extension of us, a fantastic reality,

It is a perfect combination of mind and gears.

It celebrates man and machine, that deep connection,

That unique symbiosis, that ageless fusion,

The car is a vision, a boundless love,

It is an ode to life, a road, a truth.

In line, noise, color and soul,

The machine lives, challenges, runs and calls,

It is an ongoing adventure, it is a daring challenge,

The car is poetry, an art, an embracing passion.

Mandalas

How beautiful are the mandalas

It is really true

That they work

As a stress reliever.

You have to be careful

A like

Match

The colors

Otherwise it comes out lousy

So

occasionally

you have to freeze

And choose

Pastels

With care.

How beautiful are the mandalas

It is really true

That they work

As a stress reliever.

You have to be careful

A like

Match

The colors

Otherwise it comes out lousy

So

occasionally

you have to freeze

And choose

Pastels

With care.

Mouthful

No mumbling

I repeated

The road is long

Sacrifices he makes none

Travel

Right and left

And in the end

He does the crybaby

But darling

But what the is?

Ah yes

The voice recorder.

Yes because I say.

What the heck.

I remained

Also at the dinner.

No mumbling

I repeated

The road is long

Sacrifices he makes none

Travel

Right and left

And in the end

He does the crybaby

But darling

But what the is?

Ah yes

Voice recorder.

Yes because I say.

What the heck.

I remained

Also at the dinner.

I have chills all over my body

I went down

Not thinking

That it could be cold.

Cabbage

It freezes,

I have chills

Throughout the body.

Now I turn on

A ball

The heating

But it will take

A full half hour

To stop shaking

And chattering of teeth.

I went down

Not thinking

That it could be cold.

Cabbage

It freezes,

I have chills

Throughout the body.

Now I turn on

A ball

The heating

But it will take

A full half hour

To stop shaking

And chattering of teeth.

Christmas

Under a starry sky on a clear night,

The lights are coming on, Christmas is approaching,

In homes and hearts, in every street, every scene,

A love is breathed, a special hymn is sung.

Trees adorned, with brightly colored orbs,

Gifts wrapped, with care and affection,

Excited children, eyes big and dreamy,

Christmas is an enchantment, a perfect time.

At the table gathered, families and close friends,

Food is shared, life is toasted,

Stories and laughter, true and clear connections,

Christmas is an embrace, a shared joy.

In the church resounds, an angelic choir,

Songs of peace, prayers of love,

Christmas is a message, a harmonious invitation,

To look beyond, to believe in the heart.

In gestures of kindness, in sweet words,

In giving without waiting, in receiving with gratitude,

Christmas lives, talks, embraces and touches,

It is a pure feeling, a magical virtue.

It's not just a day, it's not just a party,

Christmas is a spirit, an eternal philosophy,

It is a call to humanity, to honest goodness,

An ode to friendship, an inner light.

Celebrate Christmas, not just with gifts,

But with love, with presence, with a sincere smile,

Christmas is a gift, a moment without equal,

It is a universal embrace, a true love.

In lights, songs, smiles and soul,

Christmas lives, sings, loves and calls,

It is a continuous celebration, it is an immense joy,

Christmas is poetry, an art, a warmth that enchants.

My mansion

In the calm of a street, next to an old tree,

The house stands, a nest, a beating heart,

Walls that guard, memories and whispers of the past,

It is a warm embrace, a constant refuge.

The windows smile, the floors tell,

Every corner is a secret, every room is a friend,

Home is a companion, silent and in love,

A place of peace, a shared love.

In the kitchen they mingle, aromas and laughter,

Family recipes, secrets and traditions,

The house is a theater, an animated scene,

A stage of life, a song of emotions.

On silent nights, under a protective roof,

The home watches over, cradles and comforts,

It is a beacon in the dark, a positive warmth,

An eternal bond, a supporting force.

But the house is not only, walls and bricks,

It is a living soul, a pure feeling,

It is an invisible link, between generations and people,

Everlasting love, a secure future.

Celebrate the home, not as a thing,

But as a being, as a presence,

It is a precious treasure, a fragrant rose,

A life essence, a magical essence.

In voices, steps, touches and soul,

The house lives, listens, speaks and calls,

It is a perfect refuge; it is an endless joy,

Home is poetry, an art, an embracing love.

We put in the olives

We can

Also put

Olives,

Honey,

Then I was

Very sincere

And they

have unbuttoned themselves

To their detriment

Then do

As you wish

But I know the situation

We can

Also put

Olives,

Honey,

Then I was

Very sincere

And they

have unbuttoned themselves

To their detriment

Then do

As you wish

But I know the situation.

Killer Scissor

The umbrella is open

The umbrella is closed

Ichi

But why do you smell the books?

What is this news?

Rain

Beats on the glass

Get the scissors

And cut off the dried petals

Cut Cut

She makes the killer scissors

You laugh

The moon is full.

Oh God

What a laugh love.

The umbrella is open

The umbrella is closed

Ichi

But why do you smell the books?

What is this news?

Rain

Beats on the glass

Get the scissors

And cut off the dried petals

Cut Cut

She makes the killer scissors

You laugh

The moon is full.

Oh God

What a laugh love.

In school

In lively classrooms, between desks and blackboards,

A world opens up, a dream develops,

School is a journey, an endless adventure,

A sea of knowledge, a flowing river.

Masters and students, in a harmonious dance,

They discover together, they grow, they become enlightened,

The school is a garden, flowering and curious,

A place of discovery, where talents blossom.

Friendships are born, bonds are formed,

Laughter resounds, glances cross,

The school is a family, a cozy nest,

A fire that warms, an energy that brings one closer.

Life lessons, pages of wisdom,

Math and literature, science and art,

The school is a picture, colorful and intense,

A mosaic of ideas, a workshop of heart.

Not just books, not just exams,

School is much more, it is a gymnasium of soul,

It is a testing ground, a constant challenge,

An invitation to grow, to become a person.

It celebrates the school, not only as a building,

But as a sacred place, as a temple of the future,

It is a precious gift, a light in the path,

A key that opens, a path to the pure.

In words, hands, eyes and soul,

The school lives, breathes, teaches and calls.

The warm winter

In the frosty night where winter murmurs,

And the wind plays among bare, quiet branches,

Inside the walls of the house, in a safe corner,

Under the warm blankets lies a secret world.

A gentle warmth, a silent embrace,

The blankets whisper, caress and welcome,

It is a nest of warmth, an indulgent smile,

A haven of love, where dreams unfold.

There, between soft sheets and fluffy pillows,

Time stands still, and the soul breathes,

The outside world fades away, and everything becomes peaceful,

Just the heartbeat, a pure and clear melody.

Outside the snow is falling, white and light,

But inside that bed, only warmth and peace,

It is an eternal embrace, a sincere caress,

An intimate dance, a sweet and tenacious encounter.

Every thought subsides, every anxiety melts away,

In the warmth of the blankets, in the silent night,

It is a journey to the self, a return to the roots,

A blessed stop, a precious pause.

Celebrate that moment, that winter night,

That unique warmth, that perfect feeling,

It is a simple but profound and eternal gift,

Pure beauty.

The vegetable of meditation

The vegetable of meditation

It is the artichoke

One layer after another

Yummy

Artichoke is reduced

And you meanwhile

You refine your thinking

Yummy

Here is the heart

With his stubble

When you have finished it

Have another one

Why

The vegetable of meditation

It is the artichoke

One layer after another

Yummy

Artichoke is reduced

And you meanwhile

You refine your thinking

Yummy

Here is the heart

With his stubble.

Money Money

In the hands of the world, glittering and cold,

Money dances, commands and seduces,

He is power and passion, a modern god,

A sign of success, an inducing force.

It is a means for many, an end for some,

A key that opens, a door that closes,

It is a ladder upward, a deep fall,

A fire that warms, an ice that excludes.

In the crowded streets, in the ambitious eyes,

Money murmurs, promises and deceives,

It is a shimmering dream, a dangerous illusion,

An endless race, an arcane passion.

But money is also help, it is also charity,

It is an outstretched hand, a necessary rescue,

It is an opportunity given, an improved life,

A bridge built, a love in solidarity.

He is not only evil, he is not only benign,

Money is complex; it is an eternal enigma,

It is a mirror of man, a profound lesson,

A winding path, an alternate fate.

It celebrates money, not as a god,

But as a tool, as a means to be used,

It is a neutral energy, an open choice,

A power to be managed, a talent to be tamed.

The next day

In the silence of the night, in deep sleep,

A seed of light, it begins to germinate,

It is the awakening that calls, sweet and wandering,

A new dawn, a day to embrace.

The eyes open, the mind stretches,

The body shakes, the soul smiles,

It is an invitation to life, a pure melody,

A return to the world, a love that decides.

Outside the window, the aurora whispers,

Color and promise, in a still dark sky,

It is a gentle kiss, a sincere embrace,

A joyful awakening, a secure future.

But not only in the morning, also within being,

Awakening happens, deep and mysterious,

It is an awareness, a path of light,

A path to self, a glorious journey.

Awakening of the soul, understanding of the heart,

It is an open-mindedness, a universal love,

It is seeing beyond, it is feeling deeper,

It is uniting the world, it is becoming special.

It celebrates awakening, in all its forms,

Like a divine gift, like a blessing,

It is a constant beginning, a continuous rebirth,

An art of living, a sublime lesson.

Poison Cream

volume 2

Collection of Poems

Laura Strangers

Title: Poison Cream Volume 2

Author: Laura Strangers

First edition: October 2023

The echo of silence

In a room where time stands still,

He speaks, she is silent, echo responds.

Words like arrows, they fly,

But in their eyes, insurmountable walls rise.

And between the lines of silence,

Their souls search each other in vain,

In the meanders of a lost love,

Only the echo of a broken heart remains.

The interrupted dance

In a waltz of looks, he and she,
They get lost in staggered steps,
Their hands brush against nothingness,
Searching for the melody of yesteryear.

And like leaves in the wind,
They separate for no reason,
The music continues,
But their dance is now over.

Hidden Secrets

Behind eyes veiled in mystery,

She keeps secrets deep inside.

He, trapped in his curiosity,

Try to decipher his thoughts.

But like shadows on a moonless night,

Truths remain concealed,

And in the labyrinth of their emotions,

They are lost, never finding each other.

Stormy sea

The waves of their hearts collide,
In a sea of doubt and uncertainty.
He, a beacon seeking direction,
She, a ship adrift.

In the swirls of passions and quarrels,
They seek each other out, repel each other, annihilate each other,
And in that stormy sea,
Love struggles to survive.

Invisible cracks

In a perfect picture of smiles and promises,

Cracks arise that are invisible to the naked eye.

He, obsessed with tomorrow,

She, anchored in the past.

And as the present escapes from their hands,

The cracks widen, wearing away,

Until the picture breaks down,

Revealing the wounds hidden underneath.

Suspended between two worlds

From beyond, I look back,
To the ephemeral dance called life,
Suspended between what I was and what I am,
In this limbo, I reflect.

Was life only a fleeting breath?
Every laugh, every tear, every step,
It seems now like a faded dream,
A shadow that fades into eternal light.

But even in this endless silence,
I can still hear the echo of my existence,
And I realize that life,
It was a prelude to this immortal symphony.

Beyond the veil

Beyond the veil of mortality, I find myself,

In a place where time does not exist,

Earthly fears have vanished,

And only the purity of thought lingers.

I wonder if I have lived fully,

If I left indelible traces,

Or whether, like a gentle breeze,

I went unnoticed.

But here in the peace of this realm,

I understand that every moment, every gesture,

It had a meaning, a resonance,

And now, free of burdens, I reflect clearly.

The song of eternity

Dead, I am no longer a prisoner of time,

The chains of the body were broken,

And as I float in infinity,

I listen to the song of eternity.

Past lives, choices made,

They appear as fragments of a mosaic,

And in this new perspective,

I see the beauty of imperfection.

In this silence, I speak,

Not with words, but with the soul,

And I understand that death,

It is not the end, but a new beginning.

Secret Heart

In the silence of sleepless nights,

My heart beats to the rhythm of a name,

And while the world sleeps, I dream,

Of intertwined hands and shared glances.

But in the morning, reality sets in,

And your smile, though brilliant, is not for me,

For in the intricate dance of desires,

My love is an unheard melody.

I see you, with her, happy and carefree,

And every laugh shared, every glance exchanged,

It is a knife in my secret heart,

Where passion burns but remains unexpressed.

Invisible to your eyes

In a crowded room, this is it,

You, shining like the summer sun,

Me, a shadow following you,

Invisible to your eyes, but burning in your heart.

And as you get closer, my breathing stops,

But you pass by, chased by your thoughts,

And in your world, I don't exist,

Unrequited love, a hidden secret.

Yet, when the world goes out,

In my dreams, you are mine alone,

But with the dawn, reality returns,

And my love remains a silent echo.

Forbidden love

On starry nights, you and I,

We walk side by side,

But between us, an invisible gulf,

A forbidden love, an unconfessed passion.

Me, woman in love with another woman,

In a world that does not understand, that does not accept,

And as my heart cries out its desire,

Words remain imprisoned, unheard.

In this society, where loving is a right denied,

I dream of a world where love wins,

Your name in the wind

Every evening, at sunset, on the balcony,

I look at the horizon and whisper your name,

And the wind carries it away, to distant places,

Where my love can find refuge.

You, a man who loves another man,

Me, hopelessly in love with you,

And in this cruel game of fate,

My heart bleeds, silently.

And as the world celebrates love,

Mine remains a secret,

A whisper in the wind,

A wish never fulfilled.

Between the threads of fate

In the midst of the crowd, our gazes meet,

A suspended moment, an eternity,

But as my heart falls in love,

Yours, indifferent, continues on its way.

And I wonder, as time goes by,

If fate ever brought us together,

Or if I'm just a bystander,

In a love story that never began.

And as the world dances to the rhythm of love,

I stand by, wishing,

That among the tangled threads of fate,

May our love one day flourish.

Distorted reflection

In every mirror, I look for a sign,
A confirmation, an answer.
But every reflected image,
It tells of a restless heart.

I love you with a silent love,
But your gaze flies elsewhere,
Toward another, a man like you,
And I, a woman, remain in the shadows, unheard.

The moon's lament

The moon, pale and lonely,

Light up my night soul,

As I think of you, shining woman,

Whose passion burns for another.

I am your friend, your confidant,

But in my heart, an unconfessed desire,

Of being more than just a shelter,

To be the sun that illuminates your days.

Secret garden

In the secret garden of my heart,

Love roses bloom, red and burning.

But these roses are poisoned,

From a love that cannot, must not exist.

You are my best friend, my everything,

And every laugh shared, every secret revealed,

It fuels this forbidden flame,

Burning, silent, in the night.

That bursts, overbearingly, into me.

Tracks on the shoreline

I walk on the beach, leaving tracks,

That the wave, jealous, erases.

Like the wave, you also pass,

Leaving me alone with a broken heart.

Man, in love with a man,

In a world still struggling to understand,

That love is universal, without barriers,

Yet, my love for you remains an unrealized dream.

Toward the horizon

I look at the horizon, vast and infinite,
And in that vastness, I see the two of us,
Me, in love with you, and you, searching for yourself,
On an endless journey with no answers.

I wish to be the compass that guides you,
The beacon that lights your way,
But in the labyrinth of your feelings,
My love remains an untraveled path.
Around the big table, in a cozy room,
The family gathers, in a sweet and smiling moment,
Father, mother, children, grandparents, in a circle of love,
Food, laughter, and warmth are shared.

Hands prepare, in the laborious kitchen,
Fragrant dishes, tasty recipes,
Each dish is a language, a sincere message,
A bond, a history, a true affection.

Soul Station

The station teems, throbbing heart of steel,

Where a thousand destinies cross and then vanish.

Every track is a story, every train a farewell,

And in the crowd, eyes searching, hands clasping.

Lovers coming together in an embrace,

As the scoreboard marks a delay, a wait.

A stolen kiss under the antique clock,

A greeting, a promise, a silent tear.

In the station, every moment is ephemeral,

A meeting, a separation, a departing dream,

And as trains come and go, in a perpetual whirlwind,

Stories remain, etched on stones, in the heart of the city.

The Beat of the Station

Lights flicker in the station night,

Where life flows like trains on rails.

Hurried steps, heavy suitcases, and in between,

A soaring melody of love, fleeting and pure.

She, in a red coat, he in a black hat,

They are at platform seven, the universe seems to stand still.

But like the hands of the clock, time does not wait,

And soon, the train whistle breaks their embrace.

And so, between arrivals and departures, loves that bloom and
fade,

The station bears witness to the eternal cycle of life,

Where every goodbye brings with it the hope of a new meeting.

Under the Dome of Time

Under the grand dome of the station,

Where time seems suspended, life dances.

Every moment is a painting, every sound a song,

And among the human tide, lovers poised between joy and distance.

A soldier returning, a mother leaving,

And in between, two young people, lost in their own world.

Their hands speak more than words, telling of art,

But every train that leaves is a chapter, a new second.

In the echo of the station, stories intertwine and unravel,

Enduring loves, shattering dreams,

And as the tracks lead far below that dome,

Every soul seeks its star, in the great theater of life.

The Shadow in the Night

In the darkness, a stealthy step,
A hidden sigh, a rebellious heart,
The shadow moves, silent and deadly,
A criminal, a wolf among sheep.

In the dark alleys, plots are woven,
As the moon hides his face,
And while the city sleeps, oblivious,
He dances in the game of risk.

The Thief of Destinies

With deft hands and a sharp gaze,

He stole not only gold, but also destinies,

In every theft, a piece of soul stolen,

A criminal, master of the art of silence.

But behind the mask, a hidden secret,

A wound, a wish never fulfilled,

And in every haul, the search for treasure,

That he could fill his inner void.

The Outlaw Song

Across prairies and mountains he wandered,

An outlaw, with the law on his heels,

In his heart, an untamed fire,

And on his head, the weight of a bounty.

But in his flight, a melody resounded,

The song of freedom, of a life without chains,

And although criminal in the eyes of the world,

He was a hero to those who knew his woes.

The Profile of Sin

In the crowded restaurant, a whisper,

An exchange of eyes, a plot in the air,

Among the fancy clothes, a criminal is hiding,

With the arrogance of those who know they are untouchable.

But every crime leaves a trace, an echo,

And he, too, in the shadows of the night, fears,

That his past, like a silent hunter,

One day he may return to claim his prey.

The Night Baron

In the slums of the city, he ruled,

With an iron fist and an icy gaze,

The Night Baron, criminal and king,

Of an empire built on sins and lies.

But under his armor, a crack was hiding,

A memory, a lost love, a fragility,

And as his reign prospered,

His heart, slowly, crumbled.

The Prairie Drifter

On the horizon, a lonely dot moves,

Under a broad hat, eyes scrutinizing and proud,

A cowboy rides, guardian of the prairies,

Where the wind tells ancient stories, and silence reigns supreme.

His trusty steed, step by step,

Trace paths over wild and free lands,

In the cowboy's heart, the echo of battles and loves,

And the constant desire for an ever-new horizon.

Under the Starry Sky

When the sun recedes and the moon rises,

And a thousand stars shine in the firmament,

Cowboy lights fire, lone thinker,

Remembering faces and places from his youth.

The guitar plays a sweet, melancholy melody,

And his voice soars, uniting past and present,

In the vastness of the night, only he and the universe,

And the stories that the starry sky whispers to them.

Duel at Sunset

In the dust of the old country, two shadows face each other,

The red sun blazes, a silent witness to an impending duel,

One a cowboy, the other an outlaw, eyes fixed and hands at the ready,

One movement will determine the fate of both.

Time seems to stand still, breath held,

Then the chiming of a gunshot, and one of them collapses,

The cowboy, victorious but not triumphant, salutes his opponent,

Knowing that every duel carries a burden on the soul.

Ballad of the Desert

The desert, immense and relentless,

It hides secrets and adventures in every dune,

The cowboy, tireless traveler,

Search for treasures, lost under the burning moon.

With his hat to protect him from the scorching sun,

And his gun ready to defend the honor,

He faces snakes, bandits and sandstorms,

But his real challenge is against himself, against his fears.

The Wolf's Song

On cold mountain nights, a howl resounds,
The cowboy, camped by the fire, listens attentively,
The wolf's song, wild and free, calls to him,
Reminding him of his nature, the essence of wind.

With every sunrise, every sunset, every challenge met,
The cowboy increasingly understands the call of nature,
And like the wolf, it seeks its pack, its destination,
In the vast and unpredictable land of the West.

From Shadows to Light

Once, in the deep night, it moved,

Hands dirty with crime, heart heavy with regret,

But one day, a ray of light penetrated the darkness,

And the redeemed criminal sought the way of peace.

No longer on the run, but seeking forgiveness,

Each step, an attempt to repair, to mend,

From the depths of darkness, into the light of day,

The journey of a newfound soul.

Broken Chains

The chains of the past bound him tightly,

Echoes of crimes, sighs of victims, an unbearable burden,

But one gesture, one word, one unexpected encounter,

And the chains were broken, leaving him free to redeem himself.

Now, no longer a slave to his sins,

But warrior against injustice, defender of the weak,

A criminal who found his truth,

In redemption and service to others.

Sunset and Sunrise

In the twilight of his criminal days,

The world seemed to be tinged with blood and despair,

But at the dawn of a new life, a hope resurfaced,

The colors shone, and the heart found its mission again.

No longer a prisoner of bad choices,

But creator of a bright and just future,

Redemption does not erase the past,

But it illuminates the path to a better tomorrow.

Mirror of the Soul

Every time he looked in the mirror,

He saw the face of a criminal, a loser,

But one day, that reflection changed,

And he saw a man seeking redemption, rebirth.

Each scar, a reminder of his struggles,

Each wrinkle, a testimony of time and repentance,

In the mirror of the soul, a change,

From darkness to dawn, from sin to grace.

The Untold Story

Behind every crime, an untold story,

Of pain, struggle, despair and fall,

But in redemption, a new chapter opens,

Of awakening, of love, of newfound hope.

Each page written with tears and sweat,

It tells of a criminal who chose the light,

No longer a slave to his past,

But master of his destiny, redeemed and reborn.

The Ellis Island Promise

Across the ocean, under unknown stars,

They navigated dreams, hopes and fears,

Ellis Island in the distance, promise of gold,

Italian migrants, seeking new horizons.

With suitcases full of memories and traditions,

They faced the new world with burning hearts,

America, land of opportunity, land of infinite prospects,

The echo of Italian songs resonated in the streets of New York.

The American Dream

In small apartments, between unfamiliar walls,
The American dream of a determined people was born,
Calloused hands worked, hearts prayed,
For a better tomorrow, for free and proud children.

Among bakeries and markets, Italian resonated,
A bridge between old and new, homeland and hope,
And as the sun went down over Little Italy,
The stories of Italy were being told to new generations.

The Distance

Among the crowded streets of Manhattan,
An Italian migrant looks up to the sky,
Thinking of the hills of Tuscany, the sea of Sicily,
The pain of distance, the homesickness.

Letters and photographs, links to a distant past,
Tales of family, festivals and harvests,
In a new and unfamiliar world,
Love for Italy burned eternally in the heart.

In the land of opportunity, they planted roots,
Italian families, strong and united in challenge,
With determination and faith, they built a future,
Mixing Italian traditions with American rhythm.

Children who played baseball, but spoke in Italian,
Pasta dishes and pizza, alongside hamburgers and hot dogs,
In this fusion of cultures, languages and dreams,
A new identity was born, proud and unstoppable.

Sunsets and Sunrises

At the sunset of an era, on the horizon of a new world,

Italians sailed to America, bringing with them hope,

And at the dawn of each new day, with determined steps and big dreams,

They wrote unforgettable pages in the history of immigration.

With courage and passion, they faced challenges and obstacles,

But the strength of love, family and tradition,

He guided every Italian migrant, in this epic adventure,

Celebrating them as heroes of a timeless journey.

Angels of Light

In the night firmament, among stars and comets,

They dance ethereal figures, luminous and discreet,

Angels of light, guardians of the infinite,

They watch over us, every moment, every cry.

With silken wings, and outstretched hands,

They capture dreams, fears and expressed prayers,

Invisible guardians, heavenly presences,

They illuminate the darkness, with discreet gestures.

Heavenly Messengers

From the cradle of the universe, they descend into flight,

With messages of love, and words of comfort,

Angels, emblems of grace and goodness,

They bring hope, in every reality.

Gentle voices, like summer breezes,

They whisper promises, in furtive nights.

Winged Shadows

In the twilight, when the sun gives up,

And the darkness advances, with light, slow steps,

Angels keep watch, with outstretched wings and burning eyes,

Protecting the soul when the world renders.

Like beacons in the night, they guide the way,

With their presence, all fear goes away,

Winged shadows, sentinels of the sky,

They give peace, in every single anelo.

Angelic Dreams

In the folds of sleep, in the realm of dreams,

Angels dance, weaving patterns of silver and gold,

With heavenly melodies, and light touches,

They transport hearts, beyond the boundaries of truth.

In ethereal landscapes where anything is possible,

Angels guide, with invisible hands,

And upon waking up, between sheets and pillows,

Echoes of dreams, and warm mornings remain.

Angels and Men

In a world of contrasts, joys and sorrows,

Angels descend, amid lights and colors,

Not as gods, but as brothers,

Sharing tears, smiles and sincere glances.

In every gesture of love, in every caress given,

The angelic presence, silently making itself noticed.

The Last Kiss of the Sun

The sun, in slow descent, kisses the horizon,

Coloring the sky orange, pink and deep indigo,

Every sunset, a bittersweet farewell,

A reminder that every ending brings with it a tomorrow.

In the embrace between day and night, light and shadow,

The world stands still, admiring the celestial painting,

And in that brief instant, everything seems possible,

In the golden silence of the hiding sun.

Heavenly Dance

The sky dances in fiery hues,

As the sun recedes, leaving a shimmering stage,

Shy stars appear, ready for their turn,

But the sunset steals the show, in a brilliant last act.

Clouds dressed in gold and purple float lightly,

In a silent dance, guided by the evening breeze,

And as the night advances, with promises and mysteries,

The memory of the sunset, in the heart persists.

Boundary between Day and Dream

On the border between the day and the realm of dreams,

The sunset reveals secrets in warm, soft tones,

Echoes of stories told, promises made,

They are reflected in the waters, in infused reflections.

Each sunset, a bridge between the known and the unknown,

A shift from the concrete to the magical, from the clear to the veiled,

And as darkness envelops, with its starry mantle,

The sunset remains, like a golden memory.

Melody of Sunset

The sky plays a melody, in warm and cool tones,

As the sun goes down in a slow and majestic adagio,

Notes of orange, violet and blue, blend and intertwine,

Creating a visual symphony, which the heart does not forget.

Birds return to nests, shadows stretch to the ground,

And the world, in that brief moment, listens in recollection,

The sunset song, a lullaby for the soul,

That promises peace, reflection and renewal.

Eternal Promise

As the sun disappears, leaving behind a sky on fire,

A promise is whispered to the world with every sunset we see,

That despite the storms, challenges and tears,

After every ending, there is a rebirth, a new beginning that we embrace.

Spring Awakening

Under a turquoise sky, the earth wakes up,

After the long winter sleep, cool and quiet,

Spring dances in the meadows, with light steps,

Bringing back life, color and a secret song.

Flowers bloom, timid and bold, in a chorus of tones,

While trees dress green cloaks, renewed and proud,

Every corner, every hidden fence,

It celebrates the awakening, the return of spring mystery.

Melody of Spring

The chirping of birds, a morning melody,

Greet the spring sunrise, golden and serene,

Rivers murmur songs, in a constant rhythm,

And the breeze brings scents, of jasmine and gardenia.

In the fields, poppies dance to the rhythm of the wind,

Butterflies play among the flowers in an endless dance,

Everything speaks of rebirth, of a renewed world,

Under the spell, of spring shining.

Spring Embrace

Spring comes, like a warm embrace,

Melting ice, awakening hibernating seeds,

With every ray of sunshine, every drop of rain,

Life is renewed, in an eternal and wide cycle.

Small steps through green meadows, discoveries at every turn,

The magic of nature, in full display and splendor,

With promises of fruits, of bright summers,

Spring whispers, stories of love and ardor.

Spring Landscape

Among blue skies and cotton-soft clouds,
A picture is painted, vibrant and lively,
Daisy-covered hills, flowering valleys,
The landscape sings, in tones of spring and peace.

Lakes reflect endless skies, snow-capped mountains melt,
In a world that is constantly moving, constantly changing,
But in spring, everything seems to stop, in pure contemplation,
Admiring the beauty, of creation in its perfect expression.

Spring Dream

Close your eyes, imagine a garden in bloom,

Where every step awakens scents and colors,

Roses, violets and daffodils, in an endless mosaic,

This is the spring dream, where the soul is lost and found.

Under arbors of wisteria, among arches of clematis,

Time seems to slow down, and every moment counts,

Spring, with its gentle caress, invites us,

To live, love and dream, in every little ready.

The Last Kiss of the Sun

The sun, in slow descent, kisses the horizon,

Coloring the sky orange, pink and deep indigo,

Every sunset, a bittersweet farewell,

A reminder that every ending brings with it a tomorrow.

In the embrace between day and night, light and shadow,

The world stands still, admiring the celestial painting,

And in that brief instant, everything seems possible,

In the golden silence of the hiding sun.

Heavenly Dance

The sky dances in fiery hues,

As the sun recedes, leaving a shimmering stage,

Shy stars appear, ready for their turn,

But the sunset steals the show, in a brilliant last act.

Clouds dressed in gold and purple float lightly,

In a silent dance, guided by the evening breeze,

And as the night advances, with promises and mysteries,

The memory of the sunset, in the heart persists.

Boundary between Day and Dream

On the border between the day and the realm of dreams,

The sunset reveals secrets in warm, soft tones,

Echoes of stories told, promises made,

They are reflected in the waters, in infused reflections.

Each sunset, a bridge between the known and the unknown,

A shift from the concrete to the magical, from the clear to the veiled,

And as darkness envelops, with its starry mantle,

The sunset remains, like a golden memory.

Melody of Sunset

The sky plays a melody, in warm and cool tones,

As the sun goes down in a slow and majestic adagio,

Notes of orange, violet and blue, blend and intertwine,

Creating a visual symphony, which the heart does not forget.

Birds return to nests, shadows stretch to the ground,

And the world, in that brief moment, listens in recollection,

The sunset song, a lullaby for the soul,

That promises peace, reflection and renewal.

Eternal Promise

As the sun disappears, leaving behind a sky on fire,

A promise is whispered to the world with every sunset we see,

That despite the storms, challenges and tears,

After every ending, there is a rebirth, a new beginning that we embrace.

And in that moment of transition, between day and night, between reality and dream,

The sunset reminds us that beauty exists, even in moments of farewell,

For with every setting of the sun, there is the hope of a sunrise,

An eternal promise, which heaven gives us every day.

Spring Awakening

Under a turquoise sky, the earth wakes up,

After the long winter sleep, cool and quiet,

Spring dances in the meadows, with light steps,

Bringing back life, color and a secret song.

Flowers bloom, timid and bold, in a chorus of tones,

While trees dress green cloaks, renewed and proud,

Every corner, every hidden fence,

It celebrates the awakening, the return of spring mystery.

Melody of Spring

The chirping of birds, a morning melody,
Greet the spring sunrise, golden and serene,
Rivers murmur songs, in a constant rhythm,
And the breeze brings scents, of jasmine and gardenia.

In the fields, poppies dance to the rhythm of the wind,
Butterflies play among the flowers in an endless dance,
Everything speaks of rebirth, of a renewed world,
Under the spell, of spring shining.

Spring Embrace

Spring comes, like a warm embrace,

Melting ice, awakening hibernating seeds,

With every ray of sunshine, every drop of rain,

Life is renewed, in an eternal and wide cycle.

Small steps through green meadows, discoveries at every turn,

The magic of nature, in full display and splendor,

With promises of fruits, of bright summers,

Spring whispers, stories of love and ardor.

Spring Landscape

Among blue skies and cotton-soft clouds,

A picture is painted, vibrant and lively,

Daisy-covered hills, flowering valleys,

The landscape sings, in tones of spring and peace.

Lakes reflect endless skies, snow-capped mountains melt,

In a world that is constantly moving, constantly changing,

But in spring, everything seems to stop, in pure contemplation,

Admiring the beauty, of creation in its perfect expression.

Spring Dream

Close your eyes, imagine a garden in bloom,

Where every step awakens scents and colors,

Roses, violets and daffodils, in an endless mosaic,

This is the spring dream, where the soul is lost and found.

Under arbors of wisteria, among arches of clematis,

Time seems to slow down, and every moment counts,

Spring, with its gentle caress, invites us,

To live, love and dream, in every little ready.

Beyond the Veil of Night

In the deep silence of the night,

Beyond the veil of sleep, I take flight,

I sail starry seas, dance on golden clouds,

The dream, a boundless realm, welcomes me with open arms.

Landscapes never seen, stories never told,

In this ethereal world, everything is possible and real.

Weaver of Dreams

In the shadows behind closed eyes,

A weaver works, with threads of the moon and rays of the sun,

Interweaving dreams, visions and desires,

Creating silver tapestries, on which the soul dances freely.

Each dream, a unique masterpiece,

A canvas of emotions, fears, hopes and loves,

And in waking up, as the real world calls,

The desire remains, to return to that magical atelier.

Shipwreck in the Dream

I was shipwrecked in a sea of dreams,

Where the waves tell ancient stories,

And the stars guide to hidden adventures,

In this endless ocean where everything makes sense.

The Key to the Dream

Hidden in a secret corner of the heart,

A key is found, glittering and light,

That opens the door, to the world of dreams,

Where every wish is fulfilled, and every fear is faced.

Enchanted forests, castles in the sky,

Magical creatures and time travel,

With this key, every night becomes an adventure,

And each dream, a step toward self-understanding.

Dream and Reality

In the interplay between light and shadow, true and illusory,

The dream creeps in, whispering secrets in your ear,

In this floating space, where time does not exist,

Reality mixes with fantasy in an endless ballet.

And while the outside world sleeps, still and silent,

The inner world blooms, exploding in a thousand colors,

And upon awakening, when the dream vanishes like fog in the morning,

The certainty remains, that reality is only one of many truths.

Night Embrace

In the deep heart of the night,

When the world lays down in silent repose,

The starry mantle spreads out, vast and bright,

And the night embraces the soul, in an intimate dialogue.

Under the watchful eye of the moon, silvery and full,

Whispered secrets, desires expressed in the wind,

Night, silent confidant, listens and consoles,

In its dark veil, every heart finds refuge.

Dance of the Stars

High in the firmament, stars twinkle and dance,

In an eternal ballet between constellations and galaxies,

The night offers a stage, vast and endless,

Where every star tells a story, ancient and brilliant.

Meteors whiz by, desires sent to the universe,

And in the deep darkness, light and magic intertwine.

Cricket Song

In the stillness of the night, a lone cricket sings,

Its melody resonates, a steady, hypnotic rhythm,

Each note, a celebration of the night mantle,

A call to nature, which is awakening under the stars.

Shadows dance in the trees, the breeze whispers stories,

And the cricket's song becomes the essence of the night,

A song of peace, mystery and life,

That echoes in the heart, until the rising dawn.

Lunar Reflections

On the calm waters, the moon is reflected, bright and clear,

Creating a silver path, inviting travel,

Night, with its mysteries and promises,

It shines in reflections, in a play of light and shadow.

Each wave brings with it, echoes of dreams and hopes,

And under the moon's watch, the world seems suspended,

Right now, between reality and fantasy,

The night unveils its magic in silence and wonder.

Threshold of Night

At the threshold of night, when twilight gives way,

The world is transformed, taking on soft, calm tones,

Stars appear, one by one, like gems in the sky,

And night begins its reign, silent and majestic ruler.

Creatures of the night emerge, nature adapts,

And in this domain of shadow and light, every detail counts,

Night, with its depth and vastness,

It invites introspection, dreaming and reflection.

Melodies of the Soul

In every note that resonates, in every chord that vibrates,

One finds the essence of life, the soul expressing itself,

Music, a universal language without words or boundaries,

It speaks directly to the heart, awakening deep emotions.

From tribal rhythms to magniloquent concerts,

Each melody tells a story, a moment, a feeling,

And under the sound spell, we lose and find ourselves,

In the eternal dance of music, which never stops flowing.

Cosmic Harmony

Beyond the stars, in the vast infinite space,

It resonates a music, cosmic and perfect harmony,

Every planet, every galaxy, has its own rhythm, its own song,

And the universe sings, in an endless chorus.

We, little creatures on a blue planet,

We hear echoes of this stellar symphony,

And in the music we create, we try to emulate,

The perfect harmony, which from the cosmos is given to us.

The Heartstrings

A violin sings, the bow dances on the strings,

And each vibration awakens a memory, a passion,

Music, a maker of emotions, touches the essence,

And the heartstrings respond, in a deep echo.

Sadness, joy, love, longing,

Everything manifests itself in a melody, in a simple chord,

And as the music envelops, it whispers and enchants,

The soul flies, free and weightless, on sound wings.

Sound Wave

Like a wave breaking on the shore,

The music spreads, touching every corner, every being,

With its overwhelming force, its healing power,

It brings back memories, guides dreams, and satiates the hungry soul.

In every genre, in every tone, there is a secret,

A universal message, a bond that unites,

And when the music resonates, the whole world listens,

In a moment of pure connection, of pure magic.

At the Breath of Music

Silence. Then, a note, sweet and clear, rises,
Growing into a crescendo of sounds and harmonies,
Music comes to life, like a living thing,
She breathes, feels, loves and cries, in an endless dance.

Close your eyes, let yourself go with the flow,
Feel the pulse.

Battlefield

In the field where the grass once flourished,

Now lies the weight of iron and fire,

Echoes of cries, whispers of anguish,

A soil that drinks tears and blood.

Where there was laughter, there is now silence,

Interrupted only by the whine of the wind,

War, cruel pounce of human pride,

It steals dreams, lives, and leaves only emptiness.